JavaScript for Automation:
CraftingScripts for macOS

Jesse Shanks

aquitaine publishing

Preface

My Scripting Journey

My journey into scripting on the Macintosh began when I downloaded System 7.5.2 onto my trusty Performa 638. It's incredible to reflect on how many years have passed since then and the thousands of scripts I've written since. Back in those days, my initial foray into programming was through AppleScript and JavaScript, not necessarily the easiest entry point, but the software landscape was quite different back then.

It was a natural progression from my first programming environment, HyperCard's HyperTalk language. I'd heard that AppleScript was widely used in the publishing world. My first professional encounter with AppleScript came when I used FileMaker Pro to manage a database of virtual tradeshow vendors. A coworker was a dedicated FileMaker enthusiast. During those times, creating dynamic websites was a challenge CGI was about the only option, and database connectivity was limited. So, I crafted a series of AppleScripts that queried the database and generated webpages in a designated folder for uploading to our web server. It wasn't entirely dynamic, but it worked well for the era.

At that time, my company was Mac-focused, creating CD-ROM training programs with Macromedia Director, while the internet was still in its infancy. Over time, we started doing more Windows work, and my involvement with AppleScript became more of a hobby.

In 1999, I embarked on a project called digitallyOBSESSED!.com with my wife and her brother. This was during the early days of DVDs when you could find rows of videotapes and only a few shelves of DVDs in stores. We began writing reviews and I leveraged my scripting skills to create SQL databases and dynamically generate webpages. Despite the transition to Mac OS X and changes in the Apple ecosystem, AppleScript not only survived but thrived with additions like AppleScript Object Framework and AppleScript Studio, enabling the creation of applications in AppleScript. I developed and distributed several apps, even helping my mother stay updated on DVD news by automating the process of finding and uploading articles to our website.

I maintained a website where I shared many scripts and had various scripting-related successes, although the details have become somewhat hazy with the twists and turns in the Apple world. Despite annual rumors of AppleScript's demise, it persisted within the Apple

1

operating system. I even ran a scripting website for a while, showcasing samples of my experiments. I've always been intrigued by the idea of connecting multiple applications in a workflow.

After experimenting with the JavaScript OSAX by Late Night Software, I didn't fully embrace it due to the complexities of converting AppleScript to JavaScript. JavaScript for Applications was introduced with Yosemite, and although it received criticism initially, I eventually grasped its potential and adopted the JavaScript approach. I'm still on a learning journey with it, with plenty more I want to explore.

This book has been compiled to assist others who enjoy scripting on their computers, finding pleasure and utility in controlling their machines to perform tasks. In this book, I've included scripts that I found useful and uplifting in my own work. It's impossible to list all the individuals who have contributed to my learning through articles, tutorials, notes, snippets, and advice over the years.

When one reads articles about AppleScript and Javascript for Automation, the typical takeaway is that it is for "automating repetitive tasks on the computer." Just about as dry and boring as anything could be on the computer. But this is not close to describing what these language can do as scripting tools. A better description might be "allows the connecting of applications to create a super application."

Today, there are tools like Automator and Shortcuts that simplify script creation for computers, phones, and iPads. I've had great fun and success with these modern options. Recently, I created a shortcut that allowed me to take pictures of pages and automatically extract text, saving it to a Notes file—a pretty nifty trick indeed.

Chapter 1: History of Mac Scripting

AppleScript

AppleScript (1993): Introduced with System 7.1.1, AppleScript is a scripting language that allows users to automate repetitive tasks and control applications. It is known for its natural language-like syntax, making it relatively easy for non-programmers to learn.

Automator (2005): Launched with Mac OS X Tiger (10.4), Automator is a graphical user interface for automating tasks. It uses a drag-and-drop interface to create workflows that can perform a series of tasks within and across applications.

JavaScript for Automation (JXA) (2014): Introduced with OS X Yosemite (10.10), JXA is a scripting language that allows users to write automation scripts in JavaScript, a more universally known language. It's similar to AppleScript in functionality but uses JavaScript syntax.

*Shortcuts (2021): First appearing on iOS, Shortcuts was brought to macOS with Monterey (12.0). It provides a more modern and intuitive way to create complex automations using a simple interface, integrating well with Siri and across Apple's ecosystem.

Each of these tools reflects Apple's commitment to accessibility and power in automation, offering different levels of complexity and flexibility to suit a wide range of users, from casual to professional. AppleScript and JXA, in particular, provide a scripting interface that can interact deeply with the system and applications, while Automator and Shortcuts offer more user-friendly, graphical approaches to automation.

Javascript

The history of JavaScript, an essential component of JXA, is both fascinating and pivotal in understanding the evolution of web technologies. Here's a concise overview, which could serve as a section in a book focused on JXA for beginners:

Early Days: The Birth of JavaScript
- 1995: Creation by Brendan Eich: JavaScript was created by Brendan Eich at Netscape Communications, originally named Mocha and later

renamed to LiveScript. It was designed to complement Java by enabling dynamic interactivity in web pages, a novel concept at the time.
- Late 1995: Renaming to JavaScript: Netscape renamed LiveScript to JavaScript, capitalizing on the popularity of Java, though the two languages are fundamentally different.

Standardization and Growth
- 1996-1997: ECMAScript Standardization: To ensure consistency across platforms, Netscape submitted JavaScript to Ecma International. This led to the creation of the ECMAScript standard (ES), formalizing the core features of JavaScript.
- 2000s: Broad Adoption and Evolution: JavaScript's usage exploded with the advent of AJAX (Asynchronous JavaScript and XML), allowing for dynamic content updates without reloading the entire page. This era marked JavaScript's transition from a scripting tool to a cornerstone of web development.

Major Milestones and Versions
- ES3 (1999) and ES4 (Abandoned): ECMAScript 3 added regular expressions and better string handling. ECMAScript 4 was an ambitious overhaul but was abandoned due to disagreements over its complexity.
- ES5 (2009): This version introduced JSON support, strict mode, and array methods like `forEach`, significantly enhancing JavaScript's capabilities.
- ES6/ES2015: A major update, introducing arrow functions, classes, template literals, and promises, among others, greatly modernizing the language.
- Annual Release Cycle: From 2015 onwards, JavaScript adopted an annual release cycle, ensuring gradual, consistent updates to the language.

JavaScript on the Desktop: JXA
- JXA's Introduction with OS X Yosemite (2014): While JavaScript's primary domain was web browsers, Apple introduced JavaScript for Automation (JXA) with OS X Yosemite. JXA leveraged JavaScript's syntax and capabilities, allowing for scripting and automation of macOS applications and features, a domain traditionally handled by AppleScript.

Contemporary Era: Ubiquity and Frameworks
- Frameworks and Libraries: The emergence of frameworks like Angular, React, and Vue.js, and libraries like jQuery, underscored JavaScript's versatility.

- Node.js: The introduction of Node.js enabled JavaScript to run on servers, breaking its browser-only limitation and starting the era of full-stack JavaScript development.

The history of JavaScript mirrors the evolution of the web itself, transitioning from a simple scripting language to a powerful tool that drives modern web applications. Its incorporation into desktop automation with JXA demonstrates its versatility and adaptability. Understanding this history is crucial for beginners, as it provides context and appreciation for the language's capabilities and its role in modern computing.

Userland Frontier

"Frontier" is a notable application in the landscape of Macintosh programming, particularly recognized for its pioneering role in scripting and automation. Developed by UserLand Software and initially released in the early 1990s, Frontier stands out for its unique combination of features and its influence in the evolution of scripting on the Mac platform.

Key Characteristics of Frontier
- Scripting Language: Frontier introduced its own scripting language, UserTalk, which was designed to be powerful yet accessible. UserTalk facilitated complex scripting tasks and data handling, distinguishing Frontier from other contemporary scripting tools.
- Outlining and Object Database: One of Frontier's hallmark features was its integration of an object database with an outlining interface. This allowed users to manage and manipulate structured data and scripts in an intuitive, hierarchical format, which was quite innovative at the time.
- Automation and Web Content Management: Frontier was ahead of its time in automating tasks across Mac applications and later evolved to include web content management capabilities. It played a role in early web publishing, enabling users to automate the process of creating and managing web content.
- Extensibility and Community: The application was highly extensible, with a strong community that developed a wide range of plug-ins and extensions. This fostered an ecosystem that significantly expanded Frontier's capabilities and applications.

Historical Context and Influence
- Pioneering Scripting Environment: Frontier was one of the first applications to offer a comprehensive scripting environment on the Mac,

influencing later developments in Mac automation and scripting, including AppleScript and JavaScript for Automation (JXA).
- Contribution to Web Development: Its role in web development, particularly in the early days of blogging and content management, was significant, as it provided tools for automating and streamlining web publishing workflows.

Legacy
While Frontier's prominence has waned with the advent of more modern scripting languages and platforms, its legacy in the Mac programming community endures. It is remembered as a groundbreaking tool that pushed the boundaries of what was possible in scripting and automation on the Mac, and its concepts and design philosophies can still be seen in contemporary scripting environments, including JXA.

Perl

Early Development and Philosophy
- 1987: Perl's Birth: Larry Wall created Perl in 1987 as a general-purpose Unix scripting language. It was designed to make report processing easier, merging features from several other languages like C, awk, sed, and shell scripting.
- Pragmatism and Flexibility: Perl's design philosophy emphasized practicality and flexibility. It became known for its motto, "There's more than one way to do it," reflecting its allowance for multiple approaches to problem-solving.

Rapid Adoption and Evolution
- Early 1990s: Growing Popularity: Perl rapidly gained popularity in the early 1990s, particularly in Unix and later Linux environments. Its text-processing capabilities made it a favorite for system administrators and developers.
- Perl 5 (1994): The release of Perl 5 was a major milestone, introducing features like modules, object-oriented programming, and references. It solidified Perl's place as a versatile and powerful language.

Perl and the Web
- CGI Scripting: Perl's role in the development of the World Wide Web was significant. It became the language of choice for CGI (Common Gateway Interface) scripting, enabling the creation of interactive and dynamic web content.
- CPAN (Comprehensive Perl Archive Network): Launched in 1995, CPAN became a central repository for Perl modules and scripts, greatly enhancing Perl's capabilities and fostering a collaborative community.

Challenges and Competition
- Rise of Competing Languages: In the late 1990s and 2000s, languages like Python and PHP began to gain popularity. These languages were often seen as more accessible, posing a challenge to Perl's dominance, especially in web development.
- Complexity and Readability: Perl's flexibility sometimes led to complex or obscure code, earning it the nickname "write-only language." This aspect was criticized for making code maintenance difficult.

Recent Developments
- Perl 6/Raku: Announced in 2000, Perl 6 aimed to be a major revision of the language. However, its development took significantly longer than expected. Eventually, Perl 6 was renamed Raku in 2019 to distinguish it from Perl 5.
- Continued Use: Despite the rise of newer languages, Perl remains in use for system administration, bioinformatics, finance, and other fields where its mature ecosystem and text-processing strengths are valued.

Perl's impact on scripting and web development is undeniable. Its innovative features and community-driven approach influenced many aspects of programming and paved the way for modern scripting languages. While its prominence has waned in the face of newer technologies, Perl's legacy as a versatile and powerful tool in the evolution of programming languages continues to be recognized.

Visual Basic Script

Visual Basic Script (VBScript) is a scripting language developed by Microsoft, primarily known for its association with the Windows operating system. Its history reflects its role as a scripting tool in the broader context of Windows-based automation and web development.

Emergence and Purpose
- 1996: Introduction with Internet Explorer: VBScript was introduced by Microsoft in 1996 as a scripting language for the Windows environment. It was positioned as a lightweight scripting tool, primarily intended to be used in web browsers (Internet Explorer) and for Windows-based scripting.
- Relation to Visual Basic: VBScript was derived from Microsoft's Visual Basic programming language, offering a simplified syntax and a scripting environment. This made it accessible to non-professional programmers and useful for small automation tasks.

Key Features and Usage
- Client-side Web Scripting: Initially, VBScript found its primary use as a client-side scripting language in web development, complementing HTML and CSS on Internet Explorer. However, its adoption was limited due to its lack of support in non-Microsoft browsers.
- Windows Scripting Host (WSH): VBScript gained significant traction as a scripting language for Windows automation through the Windows Scripting Host. It enabled automation of various tasks in the Windows operating system and became popular for creating logon scripts and automating routine administrative tasks.
- Active Server Pages (ASP): VBScript was also commonly used in Active Server Pages (ASP), Microsoft's server-side scripting engine. It allowed for dynamic web pages that could interact with databases and provide user interactivity.

Decline and Legacy
- Competition and Decline: The rise of more versatile and cross-platform scripting languages, like JavaScript and Python, led to a gradual decline in VBScript's popularity. Additionally, with the evolution of web standards and the increasing importance of cross-browser compatibility, VBScript's use in web development sharply decreased.
- Security Concerns: Security vulnerabilities in VBScript also contributed to its decline. Microsoft gradually reduced its support and usage in its products, citing security as a primary concern.
- End of Life: Microsoft announced the deprecation of VBScript in Internet Explorer 11 in 2019, marking the end of its mainstream use.

VBScript's history is closely tied to the Windows ecosystem and Microsoft's web technologies. It played a significant role in the early days of web development and Windows automation. However, its platform-specific nature and the rise of more powerful, versatile languages led to its decline. Today, VBScript is remembered as part of the evolution of scripting languages in the Windows environment, with its legacy continuing in the context of Windows-based automation and ASP-based web applications.

SmallTalk

Smalltalk is a programming language known for its influential role in object-oriented programming (OOP) and its unique development environment. Developed in the 1970s at Xerox PARC by Alan Kay and others, Smalltalk was one of the earliest languages to be designed around the concept of objects, classes, and methods, which are fundamental to OOP.

Key Characteristics of Smalltalk:

1. Object-Oriented: Every entity in Smalltalk is an object, including numbers, strings, and even code blocks. This pure object-oriented approach means that everything in the language conforms to the principles of objects, which send messages to each other.

2. Class-Based: In Smalltalk, objects are instances of classes. A class defines the structure and behavior of its instances. Classes themselves are also objects, and they inherit from other classes, forming a class hierarchy.

3. Dynamic Typing: Smalltalk uses dynamic typing, where types are checked at runtime rather than at compile time. This makes the language more flexible but requires more runtime checks and can lead to runtime errors.

4. Reflective: It provides powerful reflective capabilities, allowing programs to inspect and modify their own structure and behavior at runtime.

5. Integrated Development Environment (IDE): Smalltalk is not just a language but a complete environment. Its IDE includes a source code editor, a debugger, and an object inspector, all within a live programming environment where changes can be made on the fly while the program is running.

6. Message Passing Syntax: In Smalltalk, interactions between objects are done through message passing. The syntax is designed to be readable and expressive, with a focus on sending messages to objects.

7. Influential in Design Patterns: Smalltalk's design and environment heavily influenced the development of design patterns in software engineering, many of which were first identified and described in the context of Smalltalk.

8. Legacy and Influence: While not as widely used today as some other languages, Smalltalk had a significant impact on the development of later languages, such as Objective-C, Python, Ruby, and Java, especially in their adoption of object-oriented concepts.

Smalltalk was revolutionary for its time, introducing many ideas that have since become standard in software design and development. Its

9

interactive, object-oriented approach made it a valuable tool for education in programming concepts and a platform for research in computer science and software engineering.

Scripting Today

The modern landscape of scripting, both in online environments and on personal computers, reflects a dynamic and diverse ecosystem. This portrait, drawing from the histories of JavaScript, Perl, VBScript, and the Mac-specific scripting tool Frontier, showcases the evolution and current state of scripting languages.

Online Scripting: Dominance of JavaScript and Its Ecosystem
- JavaScript's Ubiquity: JavaScript, initially created for simple client-side web tasks, has become the backbone of modern web development. Its growth is marked by frameworks and libraries like React, Angular, and Vue.js, which have revolutionized how we build interactive web applications.
- Server-Side JavaScript: With Node.js, JavaScript broke out of the browser, enabling full-stack development and making JavaScript a ubiquitous presence in both front-end and back-end development.
- Evolving Standards: The continuous development of ECMAScript standards ensures JavaScript's relevance and adaptability, addressing past limitations and introducing modern programming concepts.

Scripting on Personal Computers: From VBScript to JXA
- Windows Scripting with VBScript: VBScript played a crucial role in Windows automation, offering a scripting tool tailored to the Windows environment. Despite its decline, it highlighted the demand for platform-specific scripting solutions.
- Mac Automation with Frontier and JXA: Frontier's pioneering role in Mac scripting laid the groundwork for later developments. JXA, leveraging JavaScript's syntax and power, represents a modern approach to Mac automation, integrating seamlessly with macOS and providing a rich set of capabilities for automation and scripting tasks.

The Enduring Legacy of Perl
- Perl's Versatility: Perl's text-processing prowess and its role in early web development and system administration illustrate the versatility and power a scripting language can offer. Though its prominence has waned in favor of languages like Python, its influence persists, especially in niche areas like bioinformatics and legacy systems.

Cross-Platform and Specialized Scripting Languages

- Rise of Python and Others: Languages like Python have emerged as dominant forces in the scripting world, prized for their readability, versatility, and extensive libraries. They cater to a broad spectrum of applications, from web development to scientific computing.
- Specialized Scripting Environments: Specialized scripting environments, tailored to specific platforms or applications, continue to evolve, offering more accessible and efficient ways to automate tasks and process data.

A Diverse and Dynamic Scripting Landscape
The modern scripting landscape is characterized by diversity and dynamism. JavaScript's evolution and dominance in web development, the specialized roles of languages like Perl and Python, and platform-specific tools like JXA for Mac, all illustrate how scripting languages have adapted to meet the changing needs of developers and users. Scripting languages today are more powerful, flexible, and accessible, playing crucial roles in everything from website interactivity to server management, desktop automation, and beyond. This adaptability and ongoing evolution underscore the enduring importance of scripting in the fabric of modern computing.

Chapter 2: Introduction to JXA

Welcome to the exciting world of JavaScript for Automation (JXA), where the powerful and familiar syntax of JavaScript meets the vast capabilities of macOS automation. JXA, a bridge between JavaScript and Apple's native scripting architecture, unlocks a new realm of possibilities for automating tasks on your Mac. This chapter serves as your gateway into understanding and harnessing the power of JXA, making your interaction with macOS both efficient and enjoyable.

What is JXA?

JXA (JavaScript for Automation) is Apple's implementation of JavaScript for scripting and automating macOS applications and system actions. It provides a JavaScript interface to AppleScript's Open Scripting Architecture, allowing you to control and automate most aspects of macOS, including Finder, Safari, Mail, and even third-party applications.

- Familiar Syntax: For those acquainted with JavaScript, JXA feels right at home. The familiar syntax and concepts make it accessible and powerful.
- Integration with macOS: JXA seamlessly integrates with macOS, offering a direct line to control and automate various aspects of the system and applications.
- Versatility: Whether you're automating repetitive tasks, organizing files, controlling media playback, or even creating complex workflows, JXA has the capability to make it easier and faster.

Getting Started with a Fun Script

Let's dive in with a playful script that demonstrates basic JXA concepts in an amusing way. Imagine a script that playfully interacts with your desktop, creating a new folder named "Surprise" and then telling you a joke through a dialog box. This introduces basic file handling and user interaction in JXA.

JXA Script : Fun with Folders and Jokes

```
// Access the Finder application
finder = Application('Finder')

// Create a new folder on the desktop
desktopPath = finder.desktop.folder
desktopPath.make(new Folder({ withProperties: { name:
    'Surprise' } }))
```

```
// Prepare a joke
joke = "Why don't scientists trust atoms? Because they make
    up everything!"

// Access the Standard Additions for user interaction
StandardAdditions = Application.currentApplication()
StandardAdditions.includeStandardAdditions = true

// Display a dialog with the joke
StandardAdditions.displayDialog(joke, { withTitle: 'JXA
    Joke' })
```

This simple yet engaging script illustrates the basics of JXA: accessing and controlling macOS applications, manipulating the file system, and interacting with the user. As you progress through this chapter, you'll explore these concepts in greater depth, unlocking the full potential of JXA for automating and enhancing your macOS experience.

Continuing from our introduction to JXA with the "Fun with Folders and Jokes" script, let's delve deeper into some of the key concepts it demonstrates. Understanding these will provide a solid foundation for your journey into more complex JXA scripting.

Accessing Applications
- Application Object: JXA scripts interact with applications through the `Application` object. In our script, `Application('Finder')` creates an interface to control the Finder application. This concept is central to JXA, allowing scripts to control various aspects of almost any application on your Mac.

Working with the File System
- Manipulating Files and Folders: The script demonstrates basic file system manipulation by creating a new folder on the desktop. This is done through the `Finder` object, which is used to access and modify the file system. The `make` function and the `new Folder` constructor are used here to create a new folder.

Standard Additions
- Standard Additions Library: JXA, like AppleScript, can use Standard Additions, which provides common functionalities such as displaying dialog boxes, handling files, and more. In the script, `Application.currentApplication()` accesses the current script's

13

application instance, and `includeStandardAdditions` is set to `true` to enable these additional commands.

Displaying Dialogs
- User Interaction: The `displayDialog` function showcases how a JXA script can interact with the user. This function pops up a dialog box with a custom message and title, a simple yet powerful way to convey information or receive input from the user.

Script Structure and Execution
- Running JXA Scripts: JXA scripts can be run in various environments – through the Script Editor, Automator, or even embedded within other applications. The structure of the script, with a clear declaration of objects and sequential actions, reflects the JavaScript syntax and execution model.

Error Handling and Debugging (Not Demonstrated in the Script)
- While not shown in our simple script, error handling and debugging are critical in JXA. JavaScript's `try...catch` statements and console logging methods are applicable in JXA for handling exceptions and tracing script execution.

This script, while basic, touches upon fundamental aspects of JXA – application control, file system manipulation, user interaction, and utilization of Standard Additions. As you progress, you'll find that these concepts form the backbone of most JXA scripts, enabling you to automate a wide range of tasks on your Mac. The power of JXA lies in its ability to leverage JavaScript's syntax and capabilities to interact deeply with macOS, offering a flexible and powerful tool for automation.

Using "Say"
Creating a JXA script that utilizes the "say" command is a great way to demonstrate how to control basic system functions and play with speech synthesis in macOS. The say command, a part of the Standard Additions in AppleScript, is also accessible through JXA. It enables the script to make the computer speak aloud using the system's text-to-speech capabilities.

Here's a demonstration script along with explanatory notes:
javascript

JXA Script: Fun with Speech Synthesis

```
// Access the Standard Additions for speech synthesis
standardAdditions = Application.currentApplication()
standardAdditions.includeStandardAdditions = true

// Prepare a message to speak
message = "Hello, this is Samantha speaking through your
      Mac."

// Using the 'say' command with a Siri voice
standardAdditions.say(message, {
    using: 'Samantha',    // Specify a voice
    pitch: 50,            // Set the pitch (0 to 100)
    rate: 200            // Set the speaking rate (words per
          minute)
})

// Note: Ensure that the Samantha voice is installed and
    available on your macOS system.
// Check system settings under System Voice to see
    available voices.
```

Explanation of the Script:

    Access Standard Additions:
    The script starts by accessing Standard Additions, which
contains various utility commands like say.
    Application.currentApplication() gets the current script's
application instance, and includeStandardAdditions is set to true to
enable these commands.
    Prepare the Message:
    A variable message is defined with the text that the script will
make the computer speak.
    Using the say Command:
    The say command is used to make the computer speak the text
in the message variable.
    using: This parameter specifies the voice to be used. macOS
comes with various voices (like 'Alex', 'Victoria', etc.). You can choose
any available voice on your system.
    pitch: This parameter adjusts the pitch of the voice. It can range
from 0 to 100. A lower value gives a deeper voice, and a higher value
gives a higher-pitched voice.
    rate: This controls the speaking rate (speed) in words per minute.
A higher value results in faster speech.

This script provides a basic example of how to use the say command in JXA, demonstrating text-to-speech capabilities on macOS. It's a simple yet effective way to explore how scripting can interact with system features. You can experiment with different messages, voices, pitches, and rates to see how they affect the speech output.

Readin' and Writin'

Let's break down a script script that demonstrates a complete file I/O operation in JXA into its key components, focusing on the use of the for loop and functions for a more comprehensive understanding.

1. Setting Up the Application Object:

```
app = Application.currentApplication()
app.includeStandardAdditions = true
```

- This initializes the `Application` object to interact with various system features. `includeStandardAdditions` allows the use of standard commands like file dialogs and reading/writing files.

2. Choosing the Source File:

```
// Prompt the user to select the source file
sourceFile = app.chooseFile({
    ofType: "txt",
    withPrompt: "Please select a log file:"
})
```

- This part uses a file dialog (`chooseFile`) to the user select a text file. The selected file's path is stored in `sourceFile`.

3. Reading and Splitting the File Data:

```
// Read and split the file data
myData = readAndSplitFile(sourceFile, "\n")
```

- The script then calls `readAndSplitFile`, a custom function, passing the chosen file and a delimiter (`"\n"`) for splitting the file's content into lines.

4. The `readAndSplitFile` Function:

```
// Function to read and split the file
function readAndSplitFile(file, delimiter) {
    fileString = file.toString()
    return app.read(Path(fileString), { usingDelimiter:
        delimiter })
}
```

- This function converts the file reference to a string path, then reads the file, splitting its content based on the provided delimiter (newline in this case).

5. Logging the Data Using a For Loop:

```
// Log the data to the console
for (i = 0; i < myData.length; i++) {
    console.log(myData[i])
}
```

- Here, a for loop iterates over the `myData` array. Each iteration logs one line of the file to the console. The loop continues until it has processed all elements in `myData`.

6. Choosing the Destination File:

```
// Prompt the user to select or specify the destination
    file
destinationFile = app.chooseFileName({
    withPrompt: "Please specify the destination file:",
    defaultName: "output.txt"
})
```

- This prompts the user to specify a name and location for the destination file. This is where the data will be written.

7. Writing Data to the Destination File:

```
// Write the data to the destination file
writeToFile(destinationFile, myData.join("\n"))
```

- The script calls `writeToFile`, passing the destination file path and the data to be written (the `myData` array joined into a single string with newline characters).

8. The `writeToFile` Function:

```
// Function to write data to a file
```

```
function writeToFile(file, data) {
    app.write(data, { to: Path(file.toString()),
        startingAt: 0 })
}
```

- This function writes the provided data to the specified file. It uses `app.write`, which takes the data and the file path (converted to a string) as arguments.

Summary:
The script demonstrates a complete file I/O operation in JXA:
- Reading: Selects a file, reads its content, and splits it into an array.
- Processing: Uses a for loop to iterate over the array, performing an operation on each element (logging in this case).
- Writing: Allows the user to specify a destination file and writes the processed data to it.

Each step is encapsulated in functions (`readAndSplitFile` and `writeToFile`) for modularity and reuse, showcasing a structured and organized approach to scripting in JXA.

Chapter 3: Next Steps

JavaScript is a dynamic programming language widely used for web development, but in the context of JXA (JavaScript for Automation), it finds a unique application in automating tasks on macOS. This section will explore how the fundamental elements of JavaScript are retained in JXA, providing a familiar foundation for those already versed in JavaScript.

Section 1: Understanding the Core Elements:

1.Syntax and Structure:
  -Similarities: The syntax of JavaScript in JXA remains largely the same as standard JavaScript. This includes the use of variables, data types (like strings, numbers, arrays, and objects), functions, and control structures (like `if` statements and loops).
  -Consistency: The way you write expressions, create functions, and structure your code in JXA is virtually identical to how you would in any JavaScript environment.

2.Variables and Data Types:
  -Declaration: In JXA, variables not need to be declared with keywords just like javascript. Variables can hold data of various types like numbers, strings, booleans, arrays, and objects. There are many arguments on either side on whether implicit declaration and loose typing is a flaw or a benefit to the language.
  -Example:
```
fileName = "report.txt"
MAX_FILES = 10
filesProcessed = 0
```

3.Functions:
  -Definition and Usage: Functions in JXA are defined in the same way as in JavaScript. They can be named or anonymous, and they can be used to encapsulate reusable code blocks.
  -Example:
```
function greet(name) {
    return "Hello, " + name + "!"
}
greeting = greet("Alice")
```

4.Control Structures:

-Conditional Statements and Loops: If-else statements, switch cases, for loops, while loops, and other control structures are used in JXA just as they are in JavaScript.
  -Example:
```
for (i = 0 i < MAX_FILES ;) {
  if (i === filesProcessed) {
    // Process file
  }
}
```

5.Objects and Arrays:
  -Manipulating Data Structures: The way objects and arrays are declared, accessed, and manipulated is the same in JXA. These structures are pivotal in organizing data and handling complex tasks.
  -Example:
```
fileData = {
    name: "report.txt",
    size: 1024,
    type: "text"
}
files = ["doc1.txt", "doc2.txt", "doc3.txt"]
```

Transitioning to JXA:

-Leveraging Existing Knowledge: If you're already familiar with JavaScript, you're well-prepared to start with JXA. The foundational concepts and coding practices directly apply.
-Seamless Integration: The transition to using these JavaScript basics in the context of JXA is seamless. While JXA introduces new objects and methods specific to macOS automation, the core language remains consistent and familiar.

By understanding these fundamental aspects, you can effectively utilize JavaScript's capabilities within the JXA environment, making it easier to script and automate tasks on macOS. This foundation forms the bedrock upon which more advanced JXA-specific features are built.

Section 2: Extended Capabilities Specific to JXA

While JXA maintains the core principles of JavaScript, it extends these with capabilities specifically tailored for macOS automation. This section explores how JXA builds upon standard JavaScript, offering tools and features unique to the context of automating macOS applications and processes.

1. Building on AppleScript's Legacy:
   - History and Evolution: JXA is the spiritual successor to AppleScript, Apple's longstanding scripting language for automation. While AppleScript uses a more natural language syntax, JXA brings the power of a full-fledged programming language, JavaScript, to the realm of macOS automation.
   - Enhanced Flexibility and Power: With JXA, scripters gain the flexibility and capabilities of JavaScript, enabling more complex and powerful automation scripts compared to traditional AppleScript.

2. Direct Application Interactions:
   - Scripting Bridge: JXA uses a "scripting bridge" to communicate with macOS applications. This bridge allows JXA scripts to control applications and use their specific features and data.
   - Dynamic Access: Unlike some other scripting environments, JXA doesn't require static binding to application APIs. Instead, it dynamically accesses application features at runtime, making it more adaptable.

3. Enhanced Scripting Objects:
   - Specialized Objects: JXA introduces specialized objects and methods that are specific to macOS automation, such as the `Application` object for controlling apps or the `System Events` object for system-level interactions.
   - Extended Functionality: These objects extend the capabilities of standard JavaScript, allowing scripts to perform tasks like sending emails, manipulating files, or automating user interface elements.

4. Automation-Specific Methods and Properties:
   - Custom Methods: JXA provides methods and properties that are unique to macOS and its applications. These include abilities to interact with menus, dialogs, and other UI components of macOS applications.
   - Examples:
   - Automating menu actions in an app.
   - Retrieving and modifying document properties in apps like Pages or Numbers.

5. Interfacing with Apple Events:
   - Communication Backbone: Apple Events are the backbone of automation on macOS, and JXA provides a streamlined way to create and handle these events.

- Scripting Apple Events: Scripters can use JXA to send Apple Events to applications, requesting actions or data, and to respond to events generated by applications.

6. Leveraging JavaScript Ecosystem:
   - Integration with Existing Libraries: JXA allows the use of existing JavaScript libraries to some extent, expanding the possibilities of what can be achieved in automation scripts.
   - Combining Web and Desktop Automation: This opens up opportunities for scripts that can interact both with web content (using JavaScript libraries) and with desktop applications (using JXA's specific features).

JXA stands out as a powerful tool for macOS automation by combining the versatility and familiarity of JavaScript with a suite of macOS-specific enhancements. This unique blend allows for sophisticated automation tasks that are both efficient and adaptable to a wide range of needs. Understanding these extended capabilities enables scripters to fully exploit the potential of JXA in automating and simplifying workflows on macOS.

Section 3: Object-Oriented Approach in JXA

JXA adopts an object-oriented approach to scripting, treating applications and their elements as objects. This section will demonstrate how this approach is implemented in JXA, providing examples of how to access and manipulate these objects.

Automation Objects in JXA:

1. Concept of Automation Objects:
   - In JXA, everything you interact with is treated as an object, whether it's an application, a document within an application, or even system-level components.
   - These objects come with properties (which describe the object) and methods (which are actions the object can perform).

2. Interacting with Application Objects:
   - Applications are accessed as objects, with their features and functionalities exposed as properties and methods.
   - This allows for a direct and intuitive way to automate tasks within those applications.

Example Scripts Demonstrating Object-Oriented Approach:

1. Opening a Document in TextEdit:
   - This script demonstrates how to open a specific document in TextEdit using JXA.

JXA Script: Opening a Document in TextEdit

```
TextEdit = Application("TextEdit")
TextEdit.activate()

nd = TextEdit.Document().make()
dateString = new Date().toString()
slug = "Created: " + dateString + "\n\n"

mySlug =
    TextEdit.Paragraph({font:"Noteworthy",color:"black",siz
    e:18}, slug)

content = "You write in the style of Tech Executive and
    your form is chatty and you use details that are
    informative and your use cases are \"write a tweet\"
    and your role is comedy writer. Write about the
    following: \"holy mary mother of god pray for us
    sinners\" and that's the last words of Fredo Corleone."

nd.paragraphs.push(mySlug)

para =
    TextEdit.Paragraph({font:"Noteworthy",color:"black",siz
    e:14}, content)

nd.paragraphs.push(para)
```

   - Explanation: This script creates a new document in TextEdit with specified content using font, color, and size in two entries.

2. Fetching Data from Mail:
   - This example shows how to fetch the latest unread email from the Mail app.

JXA Script:
```
Mail = Application('Mail')
unreadMails = Mail.inbox.messages.whose({ readStatus:
    false })
latestUnreadMail = unreadMails[0]
```

```
console.log('Subject: ' + latestUnreadMail.subject())
console.log('From: ' + latestUnreadMail.sender())
```

- Explanation: This script accesses the Mail app, retrieves unread messages, and prints the subject and sender of the latest unread email.

Benefits of Object-Oriented Approach:

- Intuitive Scripting: Treating applications and elements as objects aligns well with how users typically think of interacting with their computer, making scripts more intuitive to write and understand.
- Reusability and Modularity: Object-oriented scripts in JXA can be modular, meaning you can create reusable components, like functions that handle specific tasks in an app.
- Direct Manipulation: The ability to directly manipulate application objects allows for more dynamic and interactive automation scripts.

By embracing the object-oriented nature of JXA, scripters can create more expressive, efficient, and maintainable scripts. This approach leverages the inherent structure of JavaScript to interact seamlessly with the rich ecosystem of macOS applications and services.

Section 4: Scripting Additions in JXA

Scripting additions in JXA play a pivotal role in extending the core capabilities of JavaScript for macOS automation. This section explains the concept of scripting additions and provides examples of how they can be used to perform various tasks.

Understanding Scripting Additions:

1. What are Scripting Additions?
   - Scripting additions, often referred to as "osascripts," are plug-ins that extend the native abilities of AppleScript and JXA.
   - They provide additional commands and features that are not inherently part of the standard JavaScript language or the basic JXA framework.

2. Role in JXA:
   - In JXA, scripting additions enable the execution of system-level tasks and interactions with the user, such as displaying dialogs, manipulating text, and handling files and folders.
   - They act as a bridge between the script and macOS, offering functionalities that are essential for comprehensive automation tasks.

Examples of Using Scripting Additions:

1. Displaying Dialogs:
   - One common use of scripting additions is to display dialog boxes that can interact with the user.
   - Example Script:

```
app = Application.currentApplication()
    app.includeStandardAdditions = true
    app.displayDialog('Hello, this is a JXA dialog!', {
      buttons: ['OK', 'Cancel'],
      defaultButton: 'OK'
    })
```

   - Explanation: This script shows a simple dialog box with a message and two buttons, "OK" and "Cancel". The `includeStandardAdditions` property is set to `true` to enable the use of standard scripting additions.

2. Manipulating Text:
   - Scripting additions can also be used to perform operations on text, such as finding and replacing text or formatting.

- Example Script:

```
categories = ["art literature","language","science
    nature","general","food drink","people
    places","geography","history
    holidays","entertainment","toys
    games","music","mathematics","religion
    mythology","sports leisure"]

app = Application.currentApplication()
app.includeStandardAdditions = true

choice = app.chooseFromList(categories)

console.log(choice[0])
```

- Explanation: In this script, an array of categories provides a list to load into the "Choose from List" dialog. One a choice is made the choice is the first item of an array. It can be more if multiple selections are allowed.

Benefits and Considerations:

- Enhanced Scripting Power: Scripting additions significantly broaden the scope of what can be achieved with JXA, allowing scripts to perform more diverse and complex tasks.
- Seamless Integration: These additions integrate seamlessly into JXA scripts, providing a user-friendly way to access additional functionalities.
- Versatility in Automation: By utilizing scripting additions, JXA scripts can interact more effectively with the user and the system, making them more versatile and capable of handling a wide range of automation scenarios.

In conclusion, scripting additions are an essential aspect of JXA, providing the additional tools and commands necessary to perform a broader array of tasks on macOS. Understanding and effectively using these additions allows scripters to significantly enhance the capabilities of their automation scripts.

Chapter 4: Introduction: Scripting Pages with JXA

Embracing the Power of Automation in Pages

Welcome to a pivotal chapter in our journey through JavaScript for Automation (JXA) on macOS: Scripting Apple's Pages application. This chapter is dedicated to unlocking the potential of Pages, a versatile word processor and a page layout tool, through the lens of JXA. Whether you are a writer, a designer, or someone who regularly interacts with document creation and management, mastering scripting in Pages can significantly streamline your workflow.

Understanding Pages

Before delving into the scripting specifics, let's understand what Pages is. Pages, part of Apple's iWork suite, is a powerful application that blends traditional word processing with sophisticated page layout capabilities. It is widely used for creating documents ranging from simple letters to complex reports and interactive digital books.

The Role of JXA in Enhancing Pages

JXA, a macOS-specific scripting language based on JavaScript, opens up a new dimension of interaction with Pages. Through JXA, you can automate repetitive tasks, manipulate document elements, and integrate Pages into larger automated workflows. This chapter will guide you through the process of using JXA to control and automate tasks in Pages, enhancing productivity and allowing for creative automations.

Key Topics We Will Cover

- Interacting with Documents: How to create, open, and save documents, and manipulate their contents.
- Working with Text and Styles: Techniques for formatting text, applying styles, and handling fonts.
- Integrating Pages with Other Apps: Exploring how Pages can interact with other applications and services through JXA.
- Practical Scripting Scenarios: Real-world examples and case studies to illustrate the practical application of scripting in Pages.

This chapter is designed for beginners in JXA and Pages, but also offers valuable insights for intermediate users looking to deepen their understanding. Our goal is to make JXA scripting approachable and useful for anyone looking to enhance their productivity with Pages.

As we step into this chapter, remember that the journey through JXA scripting in Pages is not just about learning code it's about discovering new ways to make your work on the Mac more efficient, creative, and enjoyable. Let's embark on this exciting adventure together!

Choose a Pages Template

This script is designed to interact with the Pages application on a Mac using JavaScript for Automation (JXA). The purpose of the script is to allow a user to choose a template from a list and then create a new document in Pages using the selected template. Here's a breakdown of its functionality:

1. Initialization of Pages Application:
    - `pagesApp = Application('Pages')`: Initializes the Pages application for scripting.
    - `pagesApp.includeStandardAdditions = true`: Allows the use of standard scripting additions like `displayAlert` and `chooseFromList`.

2. Bringing Pages to the Foreground:
    - `pagesApp.activate()`: Activates the Pages application, bringing it to the foreground.
    - `delay(1)`: Waits for 1 second to ensure that Pages is active and in the foreground before proceeding.

3. Template Selection Process:
    - `templa = pagesApp.templates.name()`: Retrieves the names of all available templates in Pages.
    - `shortTempla = templa.slice(0, 10)`: Truncates the list of templates to the first 10 entries.
    - `pick = pagesApp.chooseFromList(...)`: Displays a dialog box to the user to choose a template from the truncated list. The dialog box is customized with various options like title, prompt, default item, button names, and selection rules.

4. Handling User Selection:
    - The `if(pick == false)` condition checks if the user made no selection or clicked "Reject". If so, it displays an alert saying 'No Selection'.
    - If the user makes a selection, the `else` block is executed.

5. Document Creation Using Selected Template:
   - The `makePage` function is defined to create a new document using the chosen template.
   - Inside `makePage`, it retrieves the template object based on the user's choice and then creates a new document using that template.

Overall, this script enhances user interaction with Pages by providing a custom template selection process and automated document creation. It's a good example of how JXA can be used to automate tasks in macOS applications in a user-friendly manner.

```
pagesApp = Application('Pages')
pagesApp.includeStandardAdditions = true

// Activate Pages to bring it to the foreground
pagesApp.activate()

// Wait to make sure Pages is in the foreground
delay(1)

templa = pagesApp.templates.name()
shortTempla = templa.slice(0, 10)

pick = pagesApp.chooseFromList(shortTempla, {
            withTitle: 'Template Picker',
            withPrompt: 'Pick a template',
            defaultItems: ['Blank'],
            okButtonName: 'Choose',
            cancelButtonName: 'Reject',
            multipleSelectionsAllowed:false,
            emptySelectionAllowed:true
            })

if(pick == false) {
     currentApp.displayAlert('No Selection')
}else{
     makePage(pick[0])
}

function makePage(temp){
t = pagesApp.templates[temp]
nd = pagesApp.Document({documentTemplate:t}).make()}
}
```

Creating an Immersive Environment

This script combines functionalities of the Pages, System Events, and Music applications on a Mac using JavaScript for Automation (JXA). The idea is to create an "immersive" setup of minimal application distractions for writing along with a playlist designed for encourging creativity. Its main operations include manipulating a Pages window, executing key strokes, and playing a music playlist from the Music app. Here's a breakdown of its functionality:

1. Initialization of Applications:
   - Initializes the Pages, System Events, and Music applications for scripting.
   - Enables standard additions for the Pages app to use extended scripting features.

2. Activating and Interacting with Pages:
   - `pages.activate()`: Activates the Pages application, bringing it to the foreground.
   - `fd = pages.windows[0]`: References the first window of the Pages application.
   - Various `se.keystroke` commands are executed to simulate key presses:
      - `se.keystroke('i', { using: ['option down','command down'] })`: Simulates pressing ⌥ + ⌘ + I, which opens the Inspector in Pages.
      - `se.keystroke('0', { using: 'command down' })`: Simulates pressing ⌘ + 0, which zooms the document to actual size.
      - `se.keystroke('t', { using: ['option down','command down'] })`: Simulates pressing ⌥ + ⌘ + T, to hide the toolbar.

3. Window Adjustment in Pages:
   - Adjusts the bounds of the Pages window to specified dimensions (in this case, to fill the window of a MacBook Air.

4. Music Playlist Playback:
   - Specifies a playlist name ("Oldfield") to be played in the Music app.
   - Checks if the playlist exists and throws an error if not found.
   - Retrieves the first matching playlist.
   - Enables shuffle mode in the Music app.
   - Plays the specified playlist.

This script demonstrates the versatility of JXA in automating tasks across different applications. It shows how to manipulate window properties, simulate key presses, and control media playback, which can be useful in workflows that require interaction with multiple applications simultaneously.

```
pages = Application("Pages")
se = Application("System Events")
music = Application("Music")
pages.includeStandardAdditions = true

/* Objective-C Bridge
JavaScript for Automation has a built-in Objective-C bridge
    that enables you to access the file system and build
    Cocoa applications. The primary access points for the
    Objective-C bridge are the global properties ObjC and
    $. Got this snippet from scripting legend Shane Stanley
    */

ObjC.import('AppKit')

// Get the visible frame of the main screen
mainScreen = $.NSScreen.mainScreen
visibleFrame = mainScreen.visibleFrame

// Extracting the frame details
theX = visibleFrame.origin.x
theY = visibleFrame.origin.y
theWidth = visibleFrame.size.width
theHeight = visibleFrame.size.height

// End Scripting Bridge

// Output the frame details
console.log("X: " + theX)
console.log("Y: " + theY)
console.log("Width: " + theWidth)
console.log("Height: " + theHeight)

pages.activate()

fd = pages.windows[0]

se.keystroke('i', { using: [ 'option down','command down' ]
    })

se.keystroke('0', { using: 'command down' })

se.keystroke('t', { using: [ 'option down','command down' ]
    })
```

```
winName = fd.name()
winBounds = fd.bounds()
winBoundsText = winBounds.x + ',' + winBounds.y + ',' +
    winBounds.width + ',' + winBounds.height
winZoom = fd.zoomed()

// the y value is plus 25 for the menu bar
fd.bounds = {"x":0, "y":25, "width":theWidth,
    "height":theHeight}

// Get the name of the playlist you want to play
playlistName = "Oldfield" // Replace with your playlist
    name

// Check if the playlist exists
playlists = music.playlists.whose({name: playlistName})
if (playlists.length === 0) {
    throw new Error('Playlist not found')
}

// Get the first matching playlist
playlist = playlists[0]

music.shuffleEnabled = true

// Play the playlist
music.play(playlist)

//pageText = pages.documents[0].bodyText()

console.log(winName + ' ' + winBoundsText + ' ' + winZoom)
```

Simplify a Repetitive Process

This script automates the process of exporting a document from the Pages application on a Mac to an EPUB format using JavaScript for Automation (JXA). It involves user interaction for selecting an output folder and specifying a title for the exported document. Here's an overview of its functionality:

1. Initial Setup with Pages Application:
   - `pages = Application("Pages")`: Initializes the Pages application for scripting.
   - `pages.includeStandardAdditions = true`: Enables the script to use standard additions like `chooseFolder` and `displayDialog`.

32

2. Document Selection and Retrieval:
    - `doc = pages.documents[0]`: Selects the first open document in
Pages.
    - `docName = doc.name()`: Retrieves the name of the selected
document.

3. Output Folder Selection:
    - `outputFolder = pages.chooseFolder(...)`: Prompts the user to select
an output folder where the exported file will be saved.

4. Export Title Configuration:
    - `response = pages.displayDialog(...)`: Displays a dialog asking the
user for a title for the exported document, with the default answer being
the original document's name. The dialog includes custom buttons and
an icon.

5. Title Retrieval and Export Path Setup:
    - `myTitle = response.textReturned`: Retrieves the title input by the
user.
    - `strFolder = outputFolder.toString()`: Converts the output folder path
to a string.
    - `newEpub = Path(strFolder + '/' + docName + '.epub')`: Constructs
the full path for the new EPUB file, using the original document's name.

6. Export Options Configuration:
    - The `exportOptions` object is defined with various properties for the
EPUB export such as format, title, author, genre, language, cover, and
layout settings.

7. Exporting the Document:
    - `pages.export(doc, {to: newEpub, as: exportOptions.exportFormat,
withProperties: exportOptions })`: Executes the export command, saving
the document in EPUB format with the specified properties to the chosen
location.

This script effectively demonstrates how JXA can be used to streamline
the process of exporting documents from Pages, incorporating user
inputs to customize the export settings, particularly useful for automating
publishing or document conversion tasks.


```
pages = Application("Pages")
pages.includeStandardAdditions = true
```

```
doc = pages.documents[0]
docName = doc.name()

outputFolder = pages.chooseFolder({
    withPrompt: "Please select an output folder:"
})

response = pages.displayDialog("Title?", {
    defaultAnswer: docName,
    withIcon: "note",
    buttons: ["Cancel", "Export"],
    defaultButton: "Export"
})

myTitle = response.textReturned

strFolder = outputFolder.toString()
newEpub = Path(strFolder + '/' + docName + '.epub')

    // Export options
    exportOptions = {
        exportFormat: 'EPUB',
        title: myTitle,
          author: 'Ernest Fitzgerald',
          genre: 'General Nonfiction',
          language: 'English',
          cover: false,
          fixedLayout: false
    }

    // Export to ePub
    pages.export(doc, {to: newEpub, as:
          exportOptions.exportFormat, withProperties:
          exportOptions })
```

Chapter 5: Introduction: Scripting Numbers with JXA

Fetch news data from an API and Display in Numbers

This JXA (JavaScript for Automation) script combines several functionalities, including fetching news data from an API, processing dates, and working with the Numbers application on a Macintosh system. Here's a detailed description of its various components and operations:

1. Initialization and Standard Additions:
   - Initializes an `app` object for the current application and includes standard scripting additions.

2. Date Formatting Function:
   - Defines a function `formatDateToYYYYMMDD` to format a JavaScript `Date` object into a `yyyy-mm-dd` string format.

3. Getting and Formatting the Current Date:
   - Obtains the current date and formats it using the aforementioned function.
   - Logs the formatted date to the console.

4. User Input for News Search:
   - Displays a dialog asking the user to enter a name for a news search. This dialog includes options to either perform a custom search or fetch the latest headlines.

5. Preparing the News API Command:
   - Based on the user's choice, constructs a `curl` command to fetch news.
      - If "Search" is chosen, it uses the entered name and the current date to fetch news articles related to the search term from the News API.
      - If "Latest" is selected, it fetches the top headlines for the U.S.

6. Fetching News Data:
   - Executes the `curl` command using `app.doShellScript` and parses the returned JSON.

7. Interacting with Numbers:
   - Activates the Numbers application and creates a new document using a template titled "Read the News".

8. Error Handling and Date String:
   - Checks if the Numbers document is correctly initialized and logs any error.
   - Sets a `dateString` to the current date's string representation.

9. Populating Numbers with News Data:
   - Selects the first table of the first sheet in the Numbers document and sets its name to include the current date.
   - Iterates over the articles in the fetched news data, extracting relevant details (source id, title, content, description, URL, and image URL).
   - Populates the selected table with these details.

This script is a comprehensive example of how JXA can be used to integrate web data (in this case, news articles) into a local application (Numbers) on a Mac. It demonstrates the scripting of HTTP requests, JSON data handling, user input processing, date manipulation, and interaction with Mac applications. This makes it an interesting case study for an educational book on JXA, showing real-world application and automation capabilities.

```
app = Application.currentApplication()
app.includeStandardAdditions = true

function formatDateToYYYYMMDD(date) {
    year = date.getFullYear()
    month = date.getMonth() + 1 // getMonth() returns 0-11
    day = date.getDate()

    // Adding leading zeros if day or month is less than 10
    month = month < 10 ? '0' + month : month
    day = day < 10 ? '0' + day : day

    return year + '-' + month + '-' + day
}

currentDate = new Date()
formattedDate = formatDateToYYYYMMDD(currentDate)
console.log(formattedDate) // Outputs date in yyyy-mm-dd
     format

  answer = app.displayDialog('Please enter your name', {
      withTitle: 'News Search',
      defaultAnswer: 'Nancy Pelosi',
      withIcon: 'note',
      buttons:['Cancel','Latest','Search'],
      defaultButton:3
})

if(answer.buttonReturned=="Search"){

searchTerm = encodeURIComponent(answer.textReturned)
```

```
command = "curl 'https://newsapi.org/v2/everything?q=" +
    searchTerm + "&from=" + formattedDate +
    "&pageSize=30&apiKey=[Your API Key]'"

}else{

command = "curl 'https://newsapi.org/v2/top-headlines?
    country=us&from=2019-01-15&pageSize=30&apiKey=[Your API
    Key]'"

}

jsonObj = {}

jsonObj = app.doShellScript(command)

obj = JSON.parse(jsonObj)

numbers = Application("Numbers")
numbers.activate()
t = numbers.templates["Read the News"]
numbers.Document({documentTemplate:t}).make()

if(numbers.documents[0] === undefined){
    console.log(error)
    }

    dateString = new Date().toString()
    content = "News: " + dateString

    selectedTable =
        numbers.documents[0].sheets[0].tables[0]

    numbers.documents[0].sheets[0].tables[0].name = content

    for(i = 0 i < obj.articles.length ++i){
        newsItem =
            [obj.articles[i].source.id,obj.articles[i].ti
            tle,obj.articles[i].content,obj.articles[i].d
            escription,obj.articles[i].url,obj.articles[i
            ].urlToImage]

        if(newsItem.theSource == null){
            newsItem.theSource = ""
        }

        for(j=0j<6j++){
```

```
        selectedTable.rows[i].cells[j].value =
            newsItem[j]
    }
}
```

Convert Numbers Data to CSV and then JSON for Data Exchange

This script, written in JavaScript for Automation (JXA) for macOS, performs a conversion of data from a Numbers spreadsheet to CSV format, and then to JSON. Here's a detailed description of its functions:

Initialize Numbers Application:
The script begins by creating an instance of the Numbers application. This allows for scripting and automation within Numbers.
Set Up Current Application with Standard Additions:
It configures the current application (likely the script itself) to include standard scripting additions. This is a common practice to enhance the script's capabilities, such as file handling, text processing, etc.
Create and Populate CSV String:
An empty string csv is initialized to hold the CSV-formatted data.
It selects the first table from the active sheet of the first document in Numbers. This is the data source.
The script then iterates through each row and each cell (up to 4 cells per row) of the table.
For each cell, it appends the formatted value to the csv string.
Commas are added as delimiters between cell values, and a newline character is added at the end of each row.
Output CSV Data to Console:
The CSV string is logged to the console, providing a CSV format representation of the table data from Numbers.
Define a Function to Convert CSV to JSON:
A function csvToJson is defined to convert the CSV string into JSON format.
This function splits the CSV string into lines, uses the first line as headers, and iterates through the remaining lines to create objects with key-value pairs corresponding to the headers and cell values.
The function returns a beautified JSON string representation of the CSV data.

38

Execute CSV to JSON Conversion and Store Result:
The script then calls csvToJson with the csv string as an argument.

The resulting JSON string is stored in the variable json. This script effectively demonstrates data manipulation and format conversion using JXA on macOS. It shows how to extract data from a Numbers spreadsheet, format it as CSV, then convert and format that data as JSON. This can be particularly useful for transferring spreadsheet data to a format that's more suitable for web applications or data. exchange purposes.

Chapter 6: Introduction: Scripting Keynote with JXA

Create a Presentation in Keynote

Script to create a presentation in Keynote using selected images and preset text. Here's a breakdown of its functionality:

Initialization: The script begins by initializing the System Events and Keynote applications. The includeStandardAdditions property is set to true for Keynote, allowing the script to use standard OS scripting additions.

Data Preparation: It defines a list of signs (like "Powerful and continuing nationalism") and a corresponding set of characteristics for each sign. These are stored in an array and an object, respectively.

Keynote Interaction:

Activates Keynote and prompts the user to select multiple image files through a file chooser dialog.

Creates a new Keynote document with a white theme.

Iterates over the selected images, performing the following for each image:

Creates a new slide in the Keynote document using the "Title & Bullets" master slide.

Sets the title of the slide to the first sign in the signs array.

Sets the body of the slide to the characteristics corresponding to that sign, converted to a string.

Adds the current image to the slide.

Slide Creation: For each image, the script creates a new slide with a title and bulpoints. The title is taken from the signs array (it uses the first sign for all slides in this version), and the bulpoints are the characteristics associated with that sign.

Image Insertion: Each selected image is added to the corresponding slide in the Keynote presentation.

```
key = Application('Keynote')
key.includeStandardAdditions = true

signs = ["Title Text 1", "Title Text 2", "Title Text 3"]

characteristics = {
"Title Text 1": [
"Bul1",
```

```
     "Bul2",
     "Bul3",
     "Bul4"
     ],

     "Title Text 1": [
     Bul1",
     "Bul2",
     "Bul3",
     "Bul4"
     ],

     "Title Text 3": [
     Bul1",
     "Bul2",
     "Bul3",
     "Bul4"
     ],

     }

  key.activate()

imageCount = signs.length

images = key.chooseFile({
        withPrompt: 'Please select' + imageCount + 'images
            to add',
        ofType: ['public.image'],
        multipleSelectionsAllowed: true
    })

doc = key.Document({
    documentTheme: key.themes['White']
    })

    key.documents.push(doc)

for(i=0;i<images.length;i++){

    // Create and append a new "Title & Bullets" slide.
    slide = key.Slide({
    baseSlide: doc.masterSlides['Titles & Bullets']
    })

    doc.slides.push(slide)

    slide.defaultTitleItem().objectText=signs[0]
```

41

```
        slide.defaultBodyItem().objectText=characteristics
        [signs[0]].toString()


    key.documents[0].currentSlide.images.push(key.Image({
        file: Path(images[i])
    }))

}

response = key.displayDialog('Do you want to export a
    script', {
        withTitle: 'Script Export',
        withIcon: 'note',
        buttons: ['Cancel','OK'],
        defaultButton: 'OK'
    })

choice = response.buttonReturned
scriptText = ''
for(i=0;i<signs.length;i++){
scriptText = scriptText + signs[i].toString() + '\n'
scriptText = scriptText +
    characteristics[signs[i]].join('\n')
}


te = Application('TextEdit')

    newDoc = te.Document().make()
    dateString = new Date().toString()
    slug = "Created: " + dateString + "\n"

    myText = te.Paragraph({font:"Courier
        New",color:"black",size:14}, scriptText)

    newDoc.paragraphs.push(myText)

    try {
        newDoc.save()
    } catch (error) {
        // Notify the user that there's a problem
        console.log("Error Saving file")
    }
```

Automated Presentation in Keynote

This JXA (JavaScript for Automation) script is designed to control a Keynote presentation on a Mac. The script interacts with the Keynote application, allowing the user to set a time interval for each slide and then automatically progressing through the slides. Here's a breakdown of its functionality:

1. Initialization of Keynote Application: The script starts by creating an instance of the Keynote application and enabling standard additions to access additional scripting commands.

2. Displaying an Alert for User Input: It then displays an alert with the message "Click the amount of seconds per slide." This alert offers three buttons: "Cancel", "5 seconds", and "10 seconds". The user is given 30 seconds to respond, after which the alert will give up waiting for a response.

3. Setting the Delay Amount: Depending on the user's choice, the script sets a variable `delayAmount` to either 5 or 10 seconds. If the user cancels or doesn't select an option, it displays another alert saying "No Presentation" and presumably stops the script.

4. Accessing the Current Presentation: The script obtains the first open Keynote document, which is assumed to be the current presentation.

5. Starting the Presentation: It then starts the presentation from the first slide.

6. Automated Slide Advancement: The script enters a loop, where it waits for the duration specified in `delayAmount` before moving to the next slide. This loop continues until it has advanced through all slides minus one (since it starts from slide 0).

7. Error Handling: If an error occurs while attempting to show the next slide (e.g., if there are no more slides), the script catches this exception and displays an alert saying "Presentation Interrupted" and indicates the slide number at which it stopped.

8. End of Presentation Notification: After successfully going through all the slides, it displays an alert "Presentation ended" to indicate the end of the automated presentation.

This script is useful for automating a Keynote presentation where the slides need to advance automatically at a set interval, especially in situations like kiosks, automated displays, or timed presentations where manual control is not feasible or desired. The error handling ensures that the script does not fail silently, providing feedback in case of issues during the presentation.

```
key = Application('Keynote')
key.includeStandardAdditions = true

reply = key.displayAlert("Click the amount of seconds per
    slide.", {
        message: "Play Presentation",
        as: "informational",
        buttons:["Cancel","5 seconds","10 seconds"],
        cancelButton: 1,
        givingUpAfter:30
    })
        if(reply.buttonReturned == '5 seconds'){
            delayAmount = 5
        }else if(reply.buttonReturned == '10 seconds'){
            delayAmount = 10
        }else{
            key.displayAlert("No Presentation")
        }

prez = key.documents[0]
key.start(prez,
    {from:prez.slides[0]})
slideCount = prez.slides.length

for(i=0;i<slideCount-1;i++){
    delay(delayAmount)
    try {
    key.showNext()
    }catch(e){
    key.displayAlert("Presentation Interrupted", {
        message: "Slide " + i,
        as: "warning",
        buttons:["Cancel"],
        cancelButton: 1,
        givingUpAfter:30
    })
    }
}

key.displayAlert("Presentation ended")
```

Chapter 7: More Application Interaction

Transfer Content from Safari to a new text document in BBEdit

This script is designed to interact with multiple applications on macOS using JavaScript for Automation (JXA). It focuses on transferring the name and text content of the currently active document in Safari to a new text document in BBEdit. Here is a step-by-step breakdown of its functionality:

1. Initialize Applications: The script begins by initializing references to three applications:
    - `Safari`: The web browser from which the document's name and text will be sourced.
    - `BBEdit`: A text editor where the new document will be created. The script will transfer data to this application.

2. Retrieve Safari Document Details:
    - `theName`: Retrieves the name of the currently active document in Safari.
    - `theText`: Obtains the entire text content of the active Safari document.

3. BBEdit Operations:
    - `bb.activate()`: Activates BBEdit, bringing it to the foreground.
    - `bb.make({new: "document"})`: Creates a new text document in BBEdit.
    - The script then sets the name of the newly created BBEdit document to `theName`, which is the name of the Safari document.
    - The contents of the new BBEdit document are set to `theText`, which is the text content from the Safari document.

Overall, this script serves as an automation tool for transferring data from a web page viewed in Safari to a new text document in BBEdit. This can be particularly useful for quickly saving information from the web into a text file for editing or archival purposes. The script demonstrates the potential of JXA for streamlining workflows involving multiple applications on macOS.

```
safari = Application('Safari')
bb = Application('BBEdit')
```

```
theName = safari.documents[0].name()

theText = safari.documents[0].text()

bb.activate()

// Create a new text document in BBEdit
bb.make({new: "document"})

bb.textDocuments[0].name = theName
bb.textDocuments[0].contents = theText
```

Automate the process of capturing the current content of the clipboard and creating a note in the iCloud Notes app

This script is designed to automate the process of capturing the current content of the clipboard and creating a note in the iCloud Notes app on a Mac. Here's a step-by-step description of what the script does:

Initialization of System Events and Current Application:
The script starts by accessing the 'System Events' application, which is used to interact with various system-level elements and processes.
It also initializes the current application context to allow the script to perform standard actions like accessing the clipboard.
Identifying the Frontmost Application:
It identifies the frontmost application (the application currently active or in focus) using System Events.
Capturing the Current Application Name:
The script retrieves the name of the frontmost application and stores it in a variable.
Activating the Frontmost Application and Copying Content:
The script then activates the frontmost application and simulates a "Command + C" keystroke to copy the current selection (if any) to the clipboard.
Retrieving Clipboard Content:
It accesses the system clipboard to retrieve the text that was just copied.
Creating a Note in the iCloud Account:

The script calls a custom function createNoteInICloud, passing the "iCloud" account name and the text retrieved from the clipboard as arguments.

This function accesses the Notes application, locates the iCloud account, and creates a new note. The title of the note is set to the first six words of the clipboard content, bolded for emphasis. The body of the note is the full clipboard content.

The new note is then added to the user's iCloud notes.

Displaying a Notification:

After the note is created, the script displays a notification with a custom title, subtitle, and sound, informing the user that the note has been taken.

This script is particularly useful for quickly capturing text from any application and storing it as a note in the iCloud Notes app for later reference. It automates the process of switching between applications, copying text, and creating a new note, making it a handy tool for research or information gathering tasks.

Note: For this script to run successfully, appropriate permissions must be granted to allow the Script Editor (or the running environment) to control the computer and access the necessary applications and features.

```
se = Application('System Events')
app = Application.currentApplication()
app.includeStandardAdditions = true

frontmostApp = se.processes.whose({ frontmost: true })[0]

currentAppName = frontmostApp.name()

cApp = mail = Application(currentAppName)

cApp.activate()

se.keystroke("c",{using:"command down"})

myText = app.theClipboard()

// Create the note in the iCloud account
createNoteInICloud("iCloud", myText)

app.displayNotification("Note", {
        withTitle: "Note Taken",
        subtitle: "Research Goes On.",
        soundName: "Frog"
    })
```

```
// Function to create a new note in the Notes app
function createNoteInICloud(accountName, noteBody) {
    // Access the Notes application
    Notes = Application('Notes')

    // Find the iCloud account
    iCloudAccount = Notes.accounts.byName(accountName)

    // Define the title as the first six words of the note
        body
    noteTitle = noteBody.split(' ').slice(0, 6).join(' ')
     noteTitle = '<b>' + noteTitle + '</b>'

    // Create a new note
    newNote = Notes.Note({ name: noteTitle, body:
        noteBody })

    // Add the note to the iCloud account
    iCloudAccount.notes.push(newNote)
}
```

Quickly searching for information related to GPTs of a specific topic on Bing

This script is designed to interact with the Safari browser on a Macintosh system using JavaScript for Automation (JXA). It seems that for right now, Bing offers a more exhaustive search for GPTs. Here's a step-by-step description of what it does:

Initialize the Safari Application Object:
The script starts by creating an object safari that represents the Safari application. This object is used to control and interact with the Safari browser.
Enable Standard Additions:
safari.includeStandardAdditions = true allows the script to use standard scripting additions, which are commands and features common to Mac automation scripts.
Check for Open Windows:
The script checks if any Safari windows are open (windows.length < 1). If there are no open windows, it creates a new window.
Identify the Current Window and Tabs:
The script identifies the first window in the list of open windows as the current window and then retrieves the tabs within this window.

Create a New Tab:

A new tab is added to the current window. The script adjusts the index to reference the newly created tab (newTab).

Activate Safari:

The safari.activate() command brings the Safari application to the foreground, making it the active application.

Prompt for User Input:

A dialog box is displayed asking the user to enter a search type. This input is used to define the search query.

Encode the Search Term:

The user's input is URL-encoded to ensure that it is safely and correctly formatted for use in a URL.

Construct and Set the Bing Search URL:

The script constructs a Bing search URL that includes a site-specific search for chat.openai.com/g combined with the user-provided search term. This URL is then set as the address of the newly created tab in Safari.

Overall, the script is designed to open a new tab in Safari (or use an existing window if one is already open), prompt the user for a search term, and then perform a Bing search restricted to the chat.openai.com/g site using that term. This could be useful for quickly searching for information related to ChatGPT on a specific website directly from Safari.

```
// Initialize Safari application object
safari = Application('Safari')
safari.includeStandardAdditions = true
windows = safari.windows()

if (windows.length < 1) {
newWindow = safari.Document().make()
}


currentWindow = safari.windows[0]
theTabs = windows[0].tabs,
newTab = theTabs.push(new safari.Tab())-1,
bingTab = theTabs[newTab]

safari.activate()

    response = safari.displayDialog("Enter a the type:", {
        defaultAnswer: "",
        withTitle: "GPT Search on Bing"
    })
```

```
typeSearch = encodeURIComponent(response.textReturned)

myTerm = "site: chat.openai.com/g " + " " + typeSearch

bingTab.url = "https://www.bing.com/search?q=" + myTerm
```

Creating an image prompt for text-to-image

This script is designed to interact with various applications on a Mac using JavaScript for Automation (JXA). Its primary purpose is to generate an image-related prompt, input it into a specific web page (presumably for some kind of AI image generation), and then automate the process of submitting this prompt. Here's a breakdown of the script's functionality:

1. Application Interactions:
   - Safari: The script interacts with the Safari browser.
   - System Events: Used for simulating keystrokes and other system-level interactions.
   - Current Application: Represents the script itself, enabling it to display dialogs and choose lists.

2. Image Terms and User Interaction:
   - An array `imageTerms` is defined with various keywords related to photography and image styles.
   - The script presents a list of these terms to the user through a dialog, allowing multiple selections. It also sets some default choices.
   - The user's selections are stored in `choices`.
   - Another dialog prompts the user to enter a subject, which is then stored in `subject`.

3. Constructing the Prompt:
   - The selected terms and the entered subject are concatenated to form a `prompt`.

4. Interacting with Safari:
   - The script checks if Safari is currently open to a specific URL (`chat.openai.com`). If not, it opens a new window and navigates to this URL.
   - The script then waits for a few seconds to ensure the page loads correctly.

5. Automating Browser Interaction:
   - The `prompt` is copied to the clipboard.

```
```

- The script executes JavaScript within the Safari browser to focus on a specific text area (identified by the ID `prompt-textarea`).
- After a short delay, it simulates a keystroke to paste the prompt from the clipboard into the text area.
- Finally, it simulates a keystroke to submit the prompt (presumably by hitting the Enter key, as it uses the keycode 36, which corresponds to the Enter key).

This script is an example of advanced automation using JXA, demonstrating how to interact with multiple applications, handle user input, and automate web interactions. It's tailored for users who wish to use a generated prompt in a web-based AI tool, likely for creating images based on textual descriptions. The script showcases the capability of JXA to integrate various elements of the MacOS ecosystem into a cohesive automated workflow.

```
safari = Application('Safari')
se = Application('System Events')
app = Application.currentApplication()
app.includeStandardAdditions = true

imageTerms = ["3D vector art", "watercolor effect",
    "bokeh", "adobe illustrator", "hand-drawn", "digital
    painting", "low-poly", "low-lighting", "bird's-eye
    view", "isometric style", "character-focused", "6K
    resolution", "photorealistic rendering", "using cinema
    4D", "studio", "hyper-detailed", "Close-up",
    "polaroid", "Soft", "Indoor", "Wide-angle", "iPhone X",
    "Chalk", "Extreme Close-up", "Monochrome", "Ambient",
    "Outdoor", "Telephoto", "CCTV", "Graffiti POV", "Long
    exposure", "Ring", "At night", "24mm", "Nikon Z FX",
    "Watercolor Medium shot", "Color splash", "Sun", "In
    the park", "EF 70mm", "Canon", "Oil Painting Long
    shot", "Tilt-shift", "Cinematic", "Studio", "Bokeh",
    "Gopro", "Fabric", "Portrait", "Hard Light", "Fish-
    eye", "Polaroid", "Pencil Drawing", "Product shot",
    "Back Lit", "800mm", "Wood", "Satellite", "Spotlight",
    "Macro", "Clay", "Rembrandt Light", "Silhouette Light",
    "Fill Light", "Butterfly Lighting", "Rim", "Natural",
    "Neon", "Nostalgic", "Purple neon", "Sun Rays"]

defaultChoices = ["Soft", "Indoor", "Wide-angle"]

choices = app.chooseFromList(imageTerms, {
        withTitle: "Image Prompt",
        withPrompt: "Choose parameter for your
            description.",
```

```
            defaultItems: defaultChoices,
            multipleSelectionsAllowed: true,
            emptySelectionAllowed: true
      })

terms = choices

response = app.displayDialog('Write your subject', {
        defaultAnswer: 'Walking talking Macintosh SE',
        withTitle: 'Prompt',
        withIcon: 'note',
        buttons: ['OK', 'Cancel'],
        defaultButton: 'OK'
      })
subject = response.textReturned

prompt = choices.join(',') + ',' + subject

safari.activate()

currentUrl = safari.windows[0].tabs[0].url().split('/')

console.log(currentUrl)

if(safari.windows.length==-1||currentUrl[2]!
    ='chat.openai.com'){
newWindow = safari.Document().make()
delay(2)

newWindow.url = 'http://chat.openai.com'
}

app.setTheClipboardTo(prompt)

safari.doJavaScript('promptTextarea=document.getElementById
    ("prompt-textarea")promptTextarea.focus()', {
    in: safari.windows[0].tabs[0]
})

delay(4)

se.keystroke("v",{using:"command down"})

se.keyCode(36)
```

iTunes API Download Music Information to Numbers

This script is a JXA (JavaScript for Automation) script designed to run on a Macintosh environment, and it performs several tasks, mainly focused on searching for music artists and tracks on iTunes and then displaying the results in a Numbers spreadsheet. Here is a step-by-step description of what the script does:

1. Initialization:
    - Initializes the `Application` object to work with the current application and includes standard scripting additions.
    - Creates an object `numbers` to interact with the Numbers application.

2. User Input for Search Term:
    - Displays a dialog box asking the user for a search term (defaulting to 'Bob Dylan') using `app.displayDialog`.

3. Processing the Search Term:
    - Extracts the text entered by the user and splits it into words.
    - Joins the words with '+' to create a URL-encoded search term.

4. Constructing and Executing the Search Command:
    - Constructs a `curl` command to search the iTunes API for the encoded search term.
    - Executes the command using `app.doShellScript` and parses the returned JSON.

5. Filtering Results:
    - Filters the search results to match only those entries where the 'artistName' matches the search term.

6. Preparing Numbers for Data Display:
    - Activates the Numbers application and creates a new document.
    - Selects the first table in the active sheet of the first document.

7. Setting Up Table Headers:
    - Sets the row count of the table based on the number of filtered results.
    - Defines headers for the table: 'artistName', 'trackName', 'artworkUrl100', and 'trackViewUrl'.

8. Populating the Table with Results:
   - Loops through the filtered data and populates the table rows with information about each matching track, including the artist name, track name, artwork URL, and track view URL.

This script demonstrates a practical application of JXA for interacting with web APIs and Mac applications like Numbers. It showcases how JXA can be used to integrate different functionalities, like web data retrieval and local application automation, to create a useful workflow.

```
app = Application.currentApplication()
app.includeStandardAdditions = true
numbers = Application("Numbers")

query = app.displayDialog('Search Term', {
        defaultAnswer: 'Bob Dylan',
        withTitle: 'Search',
        withIcon: 'note',
        buttons: ['Cancel','OK'],
        defaultButton: 'OK'
    })

searchTerm = query.textReturned
splitSearchTerm = searchTerm.split(' ')
encodedSearchTerm = splitSearchTerm.join('+')

command = 'curl https://itunes.apple.com/search?term=' +
    encodedSearchTerm +
    '&country=US&media=music&entity=allArtist&attribute=all
    ArtistTerm&limit=20'

console.log(command)

jsonObj = {}

jsonObj = app.doShellScript(command)

obj = JSON.parse(jsonObj)

result = obj.results

// Filter the array for objects where 'artistName' is 'Bob
    Dylan'
filteredData = result.filter(function(item) {
    return item.artistName === searchTerm
})
```

```
numbers.activate()

t = numbers.templates["FourColumns"]
numbers.Document({documentTemplate:t}).make()

selectedTable = numbers.documents[0].activeSheet.tables[0]
selectedTable.rowCount = filteredData.length+1
selectedTable.rows[0].cells[0].value = "artistName"
selectedTable.rows[0].cells[1].value = "trackName"
selectedTable.rows[0].cells[2].value = "artworkUrl100"
selectedTable.rows[0].cells[3].value = "trackViewUrl"

for(i = 1; i < filteredData.length-1; i++){
        selectedTable.rows[i].cells[0].value =
            filteredData[i].artistName
        selectedTable.rows[i].cells[1].value =
            filteredData[i].trackName
        selectedTable.rows[i].cells[2].value =
            filteredData[i].artworkUrl100
        selectedTable.rows[i].cells[3].value =
            filteredData[i].trackViewUrl
}
```

Data from a Numbers spreadsheet, convert to JSON, and then create events in the Calendar app

This JXA (JavaScript for Automation) script is designed to interact with Numbers, Calendar, and other applications on a Macintosh system. Its primary function is to extract data from a Numbers spreadsheet, convert it into JSON format, and then use this data to create events in the Calendar app. Here's a detailed breakdown of its operations:

1. Setting Up Numbers and Application Objects:
   - Initializes a `numbers` object to interact with the Numbers application.
   - Sets up the `app` object for the current application, including standard scripting additions.

2. Extracting Data from Numbers to Create CSV:
   - Selects the first table from the active sheet of the first document in Numbers.
   - Loops through the rows and cells of the table, concatenating the data into a CSV format string.

3. Displaying the CSV Data:
   - Logs the CSV data to the console.

4. Converting CSV to JSON:
   - Defines a function `csvToJson` to convert the CSV data into a JSON format. This function splits the CSV by lines, uses the first line as headers, and maps the remaining lines to these headers, creating an array of objects.
   - Converts the CSV data to JSON and logs the beautified JSON to the console.

5. Parsing JSON and Preparing for Calendar Events:
   - Parses the JSON string back into an object and initializes a date object for the current date.

6. Setting Up Calendar Events:
   - Initializes a `calendar` object to interact with the Calendar application.
   - Selects a specific calendar named "Inbox".
   - Loops through the JSON objects, creating a new event for each entry.
      - Each event is titled 'Song of the Day' followed by the track name.

- Sets the description to the artist's name and the event URL to the track's URL.
- Sets the start and end dates, marking the event as an all-day event and repeating yearly.
- The location for each event is set as 'Home'.

7. Saving the Events in Calendar:
- After creating all the events, the script saves these changes to the Calendar.

This script is a sophisticated example of how JXA can be used to bridge data between different Mac applications (Numbers and Calendar in this case), converting data formats (CSV to JSON), and automating the process of event creation in Calendar based on spreadsheet data. It demonstrates JXA's capability for automating complex workflows on a Mac.

```
numbers = Application("Numbers")

app = Application.currentApplication()
app.includeStandardAdditions = true

    csv = ''
    selectedTable =
        numbers.documents[0].activeSheet.tables[0]
    rowCount = selectedTable.rowCount()
for(j=0;j<rowCount;j++){
    for(i=0;i<4;i++){
        csv = csv +
            selectedTable.rows[j].cells[i].formattedValue
            ()
        if(i<3){
            csv = csv + ','
        }else{
            csv = csv + '\n'
        }
    }
}

console.log(csv)

// Function to convert CSV to JSON
function csvToJson(csvData) {
    lines = csvData.split('\n')
    result = []
    headers = lines[0].split(',')
```

```
    for (i = 1;i < lines.length; i++) {
        obj = {}
        currentline = lines[i].split(',')

        for (j = 0; j < headers.length; j++) {
            obj[headers[j]] = currentline[j]
        }

        result.push(obj)
    }

    return JSON.stringify(result, null, 2) // Beautify the
        JSON output
}


// Convert and output the JSON
json = csvToJson(csv)
console.log(json)

obj = JSON.parse(json)
currentDate = new Date()

calendar = Application("Calendar")

targetCalendar = calendar.calendars.whose({name: "Inbox"})
    [0]
for(x=0;x<obj.length-1;x++){
    summary = 'Song of the Day: ' + obj[x].trackName
    desc = obj[x].artistName
    track = obj[x].trackViewUrl + '&at=11l8pS'
    currentDate.setDate(currentDate.getDate() + 1)
    startDate = currentDate
    endDate = new Date(startDate.getTime() + 60 * 60 *
        1000)
    newEvent = calendar.Event({alldayEvent: true, summary:
        summary, startDate: startDate, endDate: endDate,
        description: desc, url: track, location:'Home',
        recurrence: 'FREQ=YEARLY'})

    targetCalendar.events.push(newEvent)
}

calendar.save()
```

Trivia Questions from Filemaker Pro to a Quiz

This script is a JXA (JavaScript for Automation) script for macOS, designed to interact with both FileMaker Pro and TextEdit applications to generate a list of trivia questions. Here's a detailed breakdown of its functionality:

1. Initialize FileMaker Pro Application:
    - The script starts by creating an instance of the FileMaker Pro application. `includeStandardAdditions` is set to `true` to allow the use of standard scripting additions.

2. Run a Script in FileMaker Pro:
    - It executes a script named `"Find Cats"` in FileMaker Pro. This script likely performs some operation, possibly a search or filtering related to cats within the FileMaker Pro database.

3. Set Up and Initialize Progress Tracking:
    - The script sets up a progress tracker for the operation, with a total count (`totalUnitCount`) set to 25. This implies it will process 25 trivia questions. The `completedUnitCount` is initially set to 0, and descriptive texts are provided for the task being executed.

4. Retrieve Records from FileMaker Pro:
    - The script accesses the first document in FileMaker Pro and fetches records from a layout named `"New Trivia DB"`. The total number of these records is stored in `recordCount`.

5. Function for Random Number Generation:
    - A function `getRandomNumber` is defined to generate a random number within a specified range (inclusive), used for selecting random records.

6. Process and Store Trivia Questions:
    - The script loops 25 times to collect trivia questions. For each iteration, it:
        - Updates the progress description.
        - Selects a random record using the `getRandomNumber` function.
        - Retrieves a question and an answer from the 2nd and 3rd fields of the chosen record, respectively.
        - Stores this question-answer pair in the `triviaQuestions` array.
        - Updates the `completedUnitCount` in the progress tracker.

7. Initialize TextEdit Application:

- The script then creates an instance of the TextEdit application, creates a new document, and activates TextEdit.

8. Format and Push Content to TextEdit:
   - A title is created stating the number of trivia questions and is pushed to the TextEdit document with specific formatting (font, color, size).
   - It then loops through the `triviaQuestions` array, formatting and appending each question and its answer to the TextEdit document.

The script effectively demonstrates the use of JXA for macOS to interface with different applications (FileMaker Pro and TextEdit) for a specific task: generating a formatted document of trivia questions and answers from a database. It showcases data retrieval, manipulation, random selection, progress tracking, and inter-application communication and scripting.

```
fm = Application('Filemaker Pro')
fm.includeStandardAdditions = true

fm.doScript('Find Cats')

questionsNumber = 25

Progress.totalUnitCount = questionsNumber
Progress.completedUnitCount = 0
Progress.description = 'Processing Trivia Questions...'
Progress.additionalDescription = 'Preparing to process.'

theRecords = fm.documents[0].layouts.byName('New Trivia
    DB').records
recordCount = theRecords.length

function getRandomNumber(min, max) {
    return Math.floor(Math.random() * (max - min + 1)) +
        min
}

triviaQuestions = []

for(i=0;i<25;i++){

Progress.additionalDescription = 'Processing question ' + i
    + ' of ' + 25

ra = getRandomNumber(1, recordCount)
```

```
temp1 = fm.documents[0].layouts.byName('New Trivia
    DB').records[ra].fields[2]()

temp2 = fm.documents[0].layouts.byName('New Trivia
    DB').records[ra].fields[3]()

    triviaQuestions.push({question:temp1, answer: temp2})
    Progress.completedUnitCount = i

}

te = Application('TextEdit')
nd = te.Document()
te.documents.push(nd)
te.activate()

title = questionsNumber + ' Cat Trivia Questions' + '\n\n'

nd.paragraphs.push(te.Paragraph({ font:'Trebuchet MS',
    color:'black', size:20 }, title))

for(i = 0; i < triviaQuestions.length; i++){
questionAnswer = triviaQuestions[i].question + ' [' +
    triviaQuestions[i].answer + ']'
    nd.paragraphs.push(te.Paragraph({ font:'Trebuchet MS',
        color:'black', size:14 }, questionAnswer + '\n'))
}
```

Exporting Audio from Quicktime Media

This script is written in JavaScript for Automation (JXA) for use on macOS and is designed to interact with QuickTime Player. Here's a breakdown of its key functions:

Initialize QuickTime Player Application:
The script creates an instance of the QuickTime Player application. It also enables standard scripting additions by setting includeStandardAdditions to true. This is crucial for accessing a broader range of scripting commands within the application.
Activate QuickTime Player:
The script activates QuickTime Player, bringing it to the foreground. This is necessary for ensuring that the application is ready to receive further scripting commands.
Access the Current Document:

It retrieves the first document currently open in QuickTime Player, stored in the variable doc. This implies that the script is intended to work with a video or audio file that is already open in QuickTime Player.

Specify the Export Path and Filename:

The script sets a file path (in this case, '/Users/username/Downloads/tt.mp4') using the Path object. This path represents where the exported file will be saved.

Export Operation:

The script then performs an export operation on the doc (the first open document in QuickTime Player).

The export parameters include the destination path (in:path) and the settings preset (usingSettingsPreset:"Audio Only").

The "Audio Only" settings preset suggests that the script is intended to extract and save only the audio component of the video or audio file currently open in QuickTime Player.

This script is particularly useful for automating the process of exporting the audio track from a media file in QuickTime Player, saving it to a specified location on the user's system. It demonstrates the use of JXA for controlling and automating tasks in macOS applications, in this case, to facilitate media file manipulation in QuickTime Player.

```
qt = Application('Quicktime Player')
qt.includeStandardAdditions = true

qt.activate()

doc = qt.documents[0]

path = Path('/Users/username/Downloads/tt.mp4')

exp = qt.export(doc, {in:path, usingSettingsPreset:"Audio
    Only"})
```

Chapter 8: Using JavaScript for Automation (JXA) on the Command Line with `osascript`

Introduction

JavaScript for Automation (JXA) is a powerful scripting language for automating tasks on macOS. It allows you to control and automate Mac applications using JavaScript, a language many are already familiar with.

One of the most versatile ways to use JXA is through the command line using `osascript`, a command-line tool available on macOS for executing AppleScripts and JXA scripts.

`osascript` stands for "Open Scripting Architecture script". It's a command-line utility that lets you run AppleScript and JavaScript (JXA) scripts from the terminal. This functionality is particularly useful for integrating JXA scripts into shell scripts, automating tasks, or quickly testing and running scripts without the need for a dedicated development environment.

Basic Syntax for running a JXA script with `osascript`

```zsh
osascript -l JavaScript <script_file.js>
```

Here, `-l JavaScript` tells `osascript` that the script is written in JavaScript (JXA), and `<script_file.js>` is the path to your JXA script file.

You can also execute a JXA script directly on the command line without a script file:

```zsh
osascript -l JavaScript -e 'var app = Application.currentApplication();
app.includeStandardAdditions = true; app.displayDialog("Hello from
JXA!")'
```

This example creates a dialog box displaying "Hello from JXA!".

Writing Your First JXA Command Line Script

Let's create a simple JXA script that can be run from the command line. We'll write a script that opens the Notes app and creates a new note with some text.

1. **Creating the Script File**

    First, create a new file named `createNote.js`:

    ```zsh
    touch createNote.js
    ```

2. **Script Content**

Edit `createNote.js` to include the following JXA script:

```javascript
var Notes = Application('Notes');
Notes.activate();

var newNote = Notes.Note({name: "My First Note", body: "Hello from JXA!"});
Notes.notes.push(newNote);
```

This script accesses the Notes application, activates it, and creates a new note.

3. **Running the Script**

Run the script using `osascript`:

```zsh
osascript -l JavaScript createNote.js
```

This will open the Notes app and create a new note titled "My First Note" with the body "Hello from JXA!".

Advanced Techniques

You can pass arguments to your JXA script from the command line. Modify `createNote.js` to accept a note title and body from the command line:

```javascript
var Notes = Application('Notes');
var args = $.NSProcessInfo.processInfo.arguments;
var title = ObjC.unwrap(args.objectAtIndex(3));
var body = ObjC.unwrap(args.objectAtIndex(4));

Notes.activate();
var newNote = Notes.Note({name: title, body: body});
Notes.notes.push(newNote);
```

Run the script with arguments:

```zsh
osascript -l JavaScript createNote.js "My Note" "This is a note from the command line."`
```

Error Handling

When running scripts from the command line, it's important to handle errors gracefully. You can use try-catch blocks to catch exceptions and display meaningful error messages.

```javascript
try {
  // Your script logic here
} catch (error) {
  console.log(`An error occurred: ${error.message}`);
}
```

Using `osascript` to run JXA scripts from the command line offers a powerful and flexible way to automate tasks on macOS. Whether you're integrating scripts into larger workflows, automating repetitive tasks, or simply experimenting with JXA, the command line provides a fast and efficient environment to work in. As you become more comfortable with JXA and `osascript`, you'll discover even more ways to harness the full potential of automation on macOS.

Chapter 9: Automator and Shortcuts

Automator: Desktop GUI Scripting

Automator is a software application for macOS that enables users to create workflows to automate repetitive tasks without the need for complex programming knowledge. Developed by Apple Inc., it is included with macOS and provides a simple, user-friendly way to automate actions on a Mac. Here are key aspects of Automator:

1. Graphical User Interface (GUI): Automator offers a drag-and-drop interface where users can assemble actions into a sequence to create a workflow. The interface is designed to be intuitive, even for those who have little to no programming experience.

2. Actions and Workflows: The basic building blocks in Automator are "actions," which are individual tasks. Users can combine various actions to create a "workflow" that performs a series of tasks. Actions can range from simple file manipulation (like renaming files) to more complex operations (such as image processing or PDF manipulation).

3. Variety of Actions: Automator provides a wide array of pre-built actions that cater to different applications and functionalities within macOS, such as Finder, Safari, Calendar, and Photos. Users can automate tasks related to file management, image editing, email handling, and much more.

4. Customization and Flexibility: Workflows can be customized according to user needs. Users can create workflows that are run manually, triggered by specific system events, or used as services accessible from Finder or other apps.

5. Saving and Sharing Workflows: After creating a workflow, users can save it as an application, a service, or a quick action. These workflows can be shared with others or transferred to different Mac computers.

6. Automator and AppleScript: While Automator simplifies task automation, it also supports AppleScript and shell scripting for more advanced users who need greater control and complexity in their workflows.

7. Use Cases: Common uses of Automator include batch renaming files, resizing batches of images, automating backups, creating custom folder actions, and more. It's especially useful for repetitive tasks that would be time-consuming to perform manually.

8. Accessibility and Productivity Enhancement: Automator is part of Apple's commitment to making technology accessible and efficient. It helps users save time on mundane tasks, allowing them to focus on more creative or complex work.

Overall, Automator is a powerful tool for macOS users of all skill levels to streamline their computing tasks, enhance productivity, and automate routine processes with ease. Its integration with macOS and other Apple applications makes it a versatile and valuable component of the Mac ecosystem.

Shortcuts: From the Phone to the Desktop

The Shortcuts app, available on Apple's iOS, iPadOS, and macOS platforms, is a versatile and user-friendly tool designed to automate a wide range of tasks across Apple devices. It allows users to create custom automations and quick actions, enhancing productivity and simplifying daily routines. Here are some key features and aspects of the Shortcuts app:

1. User-Friendly Automation: Shortcuts enable users to create simple or complex sequences of actions from various apps and services. These sequences, known as shortcuts, can be triggered with a single tap or voice command.

2. Integration with Siri: Shortcuts are deeply integrated with Siri, Apple's virtual assistant. Users can activate shortcuts using voice commands, making it convenient to execute tasks hands-free.

3. Wide Range of Actions: The app offers a vast library of actions that can be combined to create shortcuts. These actions can interact with built-in apps, system functions, and third-party apps that support Shortcuts.

4. Customizable Workflows: Users can customize shortcuts to suit their needs, whether it's sending a pre-written text message, playing a specific playlist, getting directions to a favorite location, or automating complex workflows involving multiple apps.

5. Gallery for Discovering Shortcuts: The app includes a Gallery where users can browse and add pre-made shortcuts. These examples serve as a starting point for users to learn and get ideas for their own custom shortcuts.

6. Cross-Device Compatibility: With iCloud, shortcuts created on one device are available across all the user's compatible Apple devices, ensuring a seamless experience whether on an iPhone, iPad, or Mac.

7. Personal and Home Automation: Beyond personal device automation, Shortcuts can also integrate with HomeKit to automate smart home devices. Users can set up automations that control their home environment based on triggers like time of day or their location.

8. Scripting Capabilities: For more advanced users, Shortcuts offers scripting actions that allow for more complex logic and control. This

includes conditional statements, variables, and loops, enabling the creation of sophisticated automations.

9. Accessibility and Efficiency: By automating frequent and repetitive tasks, Shortcuts significantly enhance efficiency and accessibility, making technology more user-friendly and customizable.

10. Routine and Task Management: Users often leverage Shortcuts for routine tasks such as morning routines, workout start-ups, or setting up work environments, streamlining their daily activities for better productivity and time management.

Overall, the Shortcuts app is a powerful tool for automating tasks, both simple and complex, on Apple devices. It opens up a world of possibilities for personalizing how users interact with their devices, all while requiring minimal technical expertise.

Resources

MDN Web Docs (Mozilla Developer Network)
- Description: Comprehensive resource for JavaScript documentation, including language reference, guides, and tutorials.
- Access: Search for "MDN JavaScript" in your web browser.

ECMAScript Language Specification
- Description: Official specification of ECMAScript, the standard upon which JavaScript is based.
- Access: Look for the latest ECMAScript specification on the Ecma International website or search for "ECMAScript Language Specification".

You Don't Know JS (book series)
- Description: A book series by Kyle Simpson, offering deep dives into JavaScript concepts.
- Access: Available for purchase online, or search "You Don't Know JS" for more information.

JavaScript: The Good Parts
- Description: A classic book by Douglas Crockford, focusing on the most effective practices in JavaScript.
- Access: Available in most bookstores and online platforms search "JavaScript: The Good Parts".

Node.js Documentation
- Description: Official documentation for Node.js, useful for understanding server-side JavaScript.
- Access: Visit the official Node.js website or search "Node.js Documentation".

Eloquent JavaScript
- Description: A book by Marijn Haverbeke, offering an introduction to JavaScript and programming in general.
- Access: Available for free online or for purchase search "Eloquent JavaScript".

JavaScript Info
- Description: An extensive tutorial website that covers both basic and advanced JavaScript topics.
- Access: Search for "JavaScript Info" in your web browser.

JavaScript Weekly
 - Description: A weekly newsletter covering JavaScript articles, news, and projects.
 - Access: Search "JavaScript Weekly" to subscribe to the newsletter.

JavaScript for Cats
 - Description: An introductory guide to JavaScript that's very beginner-friendly.
 - Access: Available for free online search "JavaScript for Cats".

Stack Overflow
 - Description: While not solely for JavaScript, it's an invaluable resource for practical coding questions and answers.
 - Access: Visit the Stack Overflow website and use the JavaScript tag for relevant discussions.

OS X 10.10 Release Notes
 - This article describes JavaScript for Automation, a new feature in OS X Yosemite.

OS X 10.11 Release Notes
 - This article describes changes to JavaScript for Automation in OS X 10.11.

Mac Automation Scripting Guide
 - There are many different scripting languages. On the Mac, the primary ones used for automation are AppleScript and JavaScript.

Introduction to AppleScript Language Guide
 - This document is a guide to the AppleScript language—its lexical conventions, syntax, keywords, and other elements.
 - It is intended primarily for use with AppleScript 2.0 or later and macOS version 10.5 or later.

These resources cover a wide range of topics from basic syntax and concepts to advanced programming techniques, making them suitable for both beginners and experienced programmers. They can also provide useful insights and examples for those working with JXA.

www.ingramcontent.com/pod-product-compliance
Lightning Source LLC
LaVergne TN
LVHW051748050326
832903LV00029B/2792